40 Best Trout Flies

Other books by the author:
Advanced Lake Fly Fishing: The Skillful Tuber

40
BEST TROUT FLIES

Robert H. Alley

Illustrations by Dürten Kampmann
Flies tied by Dale "Lobo" Barton

A *Frank* **mato**
PORTLAND

Acknowledgment

I want to thank Frank Amato
not only for the kindness of publishing
my first book but also for giving me this book idea.

About the Author

Robert Alley has been a trout fly fishing addict for many years.
He has fished for trout across the United States. He is the
author of *Advanced Lake Fly Fishing*, a helpful title
that was recently translated and published in Norway.
In addition he has written many magazine articles for
FlyFishing, and *Fly Fisherman* and other magazines.

Illustrations by Dürten Kampmann
Flies tied by Dale "Lobo" Barton
Fly Plates photographed by Jim Schollmeyer
Book and Cover Design: Kathy Johnson
Printed in Canada

Softbound 1-57188-084-4
UPC Code 0-66066-00282-2
3 5 7 9 10 8 6 4 2

Table of Contents

Introduction

I have not only arranged these 40 patterns (most found in catalogs and fly shops) into four fly types, but they are also in the order of importance for great fishing. For that reason, I discuss nymphs, then streamers, wet flies and end up with dry flies. I then, from my experience, begin with the pattern which brings me the most success. My hope is that most of your favorites are in here. It is impossible to have every favorite pattern in one book though. My intent is to discuss the very best way to fish a particular pattern. Any discussion of flies, unfortunately, is subjective to some degree or another.

Rod Weight Recommendations

Instead of repeating myself throughout this book when dealing with "ideal" rod weights for different circumstances, I'll suggest my recommendations once, here at the beginning.

Lake fishing is best with a 7 or 8 weight rod while 4 and 5 weight rods are ideal for small streams, especially spring creeks. Large tumbling rivers will require an 8 weight rod, and I think that constant use of flies larger than a size 6 will also mean a rod of that weight. Six and seven weight rods are the best all-around rods since, out West, wind is a major factor anytime of year. Anything under a 5 weight is an extra "toy" rod.

For trout, rods need not be under seven feet or over nine.

Few trout anglers need more than two outfits. A short, light rod and a long, medium weight one will do.

Chart of 40 Best Patterns

Nymphs	Streamers and Bucktails
Gold Ribbed Hare's Ear	Woolly Bugger
Gray Nymph	Muddler Minnow
Zug Bug	Marabou Leech
Beaver	Matuka
Black Midge Pupa	Light Spruce Streamer
Pheasant Tail	Zonker
Kaufmann's Stone (Brown)	Sheep Shad
American March Brown (Nymph)	Allies Chenille Coachman
Scud	Black Nosed Dace
Prince Nymph	Mickey Finn

Wets	Dries
Brown Hackle Peacock	Adams
Gray Hackle Yellow	Light Cahill
"True" Woolly Worm	Dark Cahill
Brown Woolly Worm	Bivisible
Black Woolly Worm	Irresistible
Gray-Brown Woolly Worm	Hair Wing Royal Coachman
Olive Woolly Worm	Elk Hair Caddis
Hare's Ear	Dave's Hopper
Black Ant	Black Fur Ant
Coachman	Black Midge

Nymphs

Along with woolly worms, nymphs are my "mainstay" patterns which day in and day out provide at least 70 percent of my fish-full hours. I prefer nymphs which are tied with slim tapered bodies and sparse hackles.

I consider these first three nymphs—the Gold Ribbed Hare's Ear, the Gray Nymph and the Zug Bug—to be the "big" three patterns for both lake and river fly fishing. It really is impossible to briefly summarize all of the ways that they can be possibly be used, so my purpose is to show the "best" techniques.

Gold Ribbed Hare's Ear

Tail: Brown hackle
Body: Hare's ear fur, dubbed
Thorax: Gray goose or duck
Legs: Picked out from dubbing of body
Optional: Gold ribbing (for me, better without)

If in doubt, this is the pattern to tie on the tippet at any time of day, or in any type of water condition. It is that good. The fly can resemble a wide assortment of bugs and bottom foods. I prefer it without the gold ribbing, with a slim tapered body, and with sparse hackles near the neck—particularly for lake fly fishing. The thick body style for this pattern works best in fast currents where stoneflies or caddisflies dominate and where trout can take a quick glance at their food and trout flies.

In a lake or quiet pool of a river, when the Hare's Ear is barely inched along the bottom, it resembles slow moving bugs and sometimes even a scud. In stillwaters, a Wet Cel II takes the Hare's Ear to the bottom. In moving currents, a fast sinking Wet Tip line with a five-foot leader plummets the fly to six foot depths. The same thing is accomplished with a floating line and a nine-foot leader with split shot clamped a foot above the Hare's Ear. A bead head pattern works with either line and leader combination. The bead head adds flash, an attractor element which can revive a fish-less day when working in fast currents.

These various line and leader combinations require different techniques. An upstream, cross-current cast is needed to help an unweighted fly reach the bottom whether the line is a floating or Wet Tip type. The idea is to cast well above the desired spot in order to direct the nymph toward the level of the trout. A weighted or beaded nymph can be cast straight across and then down to the spot where the trout is (or ought) to be resting. Look for mid-stream boulders, stumps, or weeds since these hold bigger trout than the same cover near the bank. The very best idea is to notice slow spots in, amidst the currents. One should always use upstream mends or make a serpentine cast to create a drag-less drift. A yarn strike indicator is often used as a "fly fishing bobber" but you only need to watch the end of the line. For me, any sort of "bobber" takes away from the original idea of fly fishing—even if I miss a few strikes!

A shallow riffle is the best place to fish with an unweighted Hare's Ear on a floating line. I like to cast slightly upstream and let the fly drift down without any line strips. Years ago, I knew someone who liked to fish the Yellow Breeches with a lightly greased Hare's Ear Nymph. He fished it with success in the film on the water. He cast it upstream and well above a rising rainbow or brown but, with a long rod, he held about 20 feet of line above the surface. Throughout the drift, he maintained tension on the line as the fly drifted toward its target. When the floating nymph nosed itself up to the feeding trout, he barely twitched it upstream. Invariably, the trout gulped it down. All of this must be done perfectly in order to work, and it is easier to write about than achieve!

I use the size 12 Hare's Ear during the *Callibaetis* mayfly hatch. On a sinking line, I jerk it along rather quickly and then toward the surface until the trout tells me I must fish it the same way near the surface.

In the summer, I use a size 16 pattern but I also carry a size 10 Hare's Ear for slightly muddy water and for other species besides trout.

In late spring and summer, it's important to consider the water temperature and its effect on trout. Below 50 degrees, they are glued to the bottom. Most species will start to move up when the water temperature rises to 55. They come shoreward until the surface water layer reaches 60 degrees and then drop back to mid-depths as the surface layer goes up to 65. Above that temperature, they are glued on the bottom once again. Brook trout head to the bottom first, near 60 degrees, while brown trout may hide in near-surface hideouts until the water reaches 68. Rainbows will return to the bottom in-between that range.

In midsummer, many anglers go home, back to town, or to other lakes or streams while their favorite place is often too warm to fish. I persist and fish those warm lakes with nymphs or Woolly Worms. Usually I crawl them ridiculously slow on the bottom—and eventually get a few. They are seldom below two pounds. I guess that I like fishing so much that I don't care to waste a weekend hopping from one place to another—yet I have moved to a second, higher lake in the afternoon or, most likely, the next day. For the best results, I have found that one should travel up, or down, at least 3,000 feet since that roughly means about a five degree difference in water temperatures. In a river, keep traveling upstream and search for faster and cooler water.

Almost invariably, especially in the summer, when the brown fly doesn't bring results, the olive one will. With my sparsely tied style, it imitates olive-colored mayfly nymphs ascending to the surface.

Maybe that is why the olive Hare's Ear does its best work in the top six to eight feet of a lake and near the weeds—even when there is no sign of a hatch.

While the deeply-sunken original Hare's Ear does its best on dead-slow retrieves, the olive-colored nymph will produce better on somewhat faster and erratic retrieves. My observation, though, is that most fly anglers fish much too quickly. Use caution.

One really doesn't need the Hare's Ear smaller than a size 16. It probably has something to do with the size of the Olive Dun and other such mayflies which are usually found in limestone, spring creeks. In these slow currents, the best way to work the nymph is with a careful upstream drift presented to a rising trout, or to a spot where one ought to be.

The black Hare's Ear silhouettes well in green-colored or dark waters. In recent years I have decided that it's better to fish a fairly small pattern (a size 12) than a larger one in discolored water. One of my mild debates near a lake came from a die-hard bucktail man who insisted that big flies were the only type to work in dirty water—until some of my brown trout were almost as big his.

The black pattern, in the same size, is often effective early in the year—usually April. A medium-slow retrieve over the rocks, and other such techniques usually work.

A good way to summarize the use of this fly is by noting the color progression: a black Hare's Ear in April, an olive one for May, and the typical brown pattern for June. The progression works this way because of the natural predominating color of insects, or bugs, throughout the early half of the trout season.

In the summer, bug life is at a minimum and I find dull shades are best fished on the bottom. The fall, at least for me, is much too variable to key into any sort of color scheme.

The Hare's Ear gained its name from the fur wound onto the shank of the hook—the Hare's Ear! Originally, early in our century, it was tied to imitate the various shades of the Theakston Blue Drake mayfly which then was sometimes referred to as the Blue Dun.

The brown Hare's Ear is the original one that Mary Orvis Marbury wrote of in her book, *Favorite Flies and Their Patterns* (as a wet winged fly). In recent years, other shades have been added and have greatly broadened the use of the Hare's Ear as a nymph.

Gray Nymph

Tail: Badger hair strands
Body: Muskrat fur
Hackle: Gray grizzle
Head: Black or brown

The Gray Nymph is another pattern which works well tied either sparsely or thickly. The latter brings better results in big, cliff-lined lakes for both trout and smallmouth bass. (Here in California, smallmouth bass often accompany rainbow trout in many of the large foothill reservoirs.)

I have found that the thick-bodied, size 12 Gray Nymph is very successful when fished slowly, along the bottom of a lake. Yet, the slimmer style works much better in small streams, whether they are lively ones with runs and riffles, or ones that take their time winding around meadows or fields. Great finesse of casting and drifting is required for stream fishing the Gray Nymph.

When I see gray-colored caddisflies hovering near the surface of a lake or stream, I tie on a sparse, size 16 Gray Nymph, let it sink about one foot and pull it toward the top of the water. At least 50% of the time, this works just fine. It seems that a major hatch requires an exact imitation while less concentrated ones make the trout less finicky. The main exception is likely to be in a spring creeks like California's Hat Creek, Idaho's Henry's Fork, Virginia's Mossey Creek or Pennsylvania's Letort.

This pattern, in a size 10 or 12, is a reasonable imitation for when the Western Gray Drake mayfly hatches. Since this mayfly often abounds in fast tumbling rivers, the standard thick-bodied style makes for better success. In slow spots, an exact Gray Drake imitation may be needed but my instinct is usually for the general-purpose pattern.

Seasonally, the Gray Nymph is important at the beginning of the year—in April and early May.

Zug Bug

Tail: Three strands of peacock herl
Body: Peacock herl ribbed with silver oval tinsel
Wing cases: Mallard flank (cut short)
Hackle: Brown
Head: Black

In the typical store-bought, thick-bodied tying style, this nymph (in a size 12) is the most reminiscent of a beetle, (or any bug) when it is crawled along the bottom of the water with zigzag jerks to the right and to the left. This pattern, and method, is often the first one to use at the beginning of the season. (Yet, the black Hare's Ear competes well with it.)

To reach the bottom, particularly in a lake, a full sinking line must be used. Most of the time, a Wet Cel II will get the fly down to

25 feet if cast about 60 feet out. If the deepest hole, in a small body of water, is no deeper than 10 or 12 feet, I would choose the Wet Cel I. Most large reservoirs have great depths though. They need the Wet Cel Hi-D line. Fly fishing will probably not be much fun if one needs a faster line for any given lake.

Roily currents or stillwaters are a cue for the Zug Bug. In a size 12, it works as an attractor, but it must be fished along the bottom at a speed a bit faster than a crawl. (The flash of a big bright streamer is usually too much for most trout in lakes or small rivers.)

In rivers, the Zug Bug is perfect for use in currents and most effective in riffles. Of the four methods that exist to get a fly to the stream bottom—Wet Tip line, long leader and unweighted fly, split shot or bead head—I prefer the leader approach because it is the most enjoyable to cast. The best way to decide what is best for you is by measuring the length of your cast. If it is under 30 feet, the bead head, or split shot methods will work well. The other methods are easier to use when making longer casts.

In shallow creeks and runs, a floating line must be used to provide a quiet presentation. In rivers with deep pools and with widths of 80 feet or more, the combination of a Wet Tip and leader may be needed. However, wind is an equalizer. West of the plains here in the United States, it is much too common. To remain a "hook-less" and unhurt angler, a Wet Tip and short leader is the only sane way to fish in such weather.

As summer heat broils the spring temperatures away, I reduce the Zug Bug to a size 16 and keep it on the bottom since that is where it does its best work. In fact, I think I can stick my neck out and say that the deeper it is fished, the better the Zug Bug will work. From my experience, I have found that it is rather ineffective from the surface on down to about six-foot depths.

On the bottom, a thicker Zug Bug (in a size 16) can imitate waterboatmen or backswimmer bugs.

In *The Complete Book of Western Hatches*, Rick Hafele and Dave Hughes write that Zug Bug nymphs can be tied to imitate damselfly and dragonfly naiads depending upon the tying style. I don't know a lot about that, but I agree with them when they write that the Zug Bug resembles different uncased caddis larvae types.

Beaver

Tail: Wood duck fiber wisp
Body: Beaver fur
Hackle: Gray partridge
Head: Brown

My greatest success with the Beaver has occurred during the fall. I like to use it in sizes 12 and 16. (In fact, very few of my nymphs for trout are any larger, yet there are some which are smaller.)

The Beaver, I have found, is outstanding in stillwaters and in the smooth currents of meadow streams. In either case, a size 16 will be the most effective because it will resemble some midges and mayflies. To imitate a midge larva, one must crawl the Beaver along the bottom. This specific method will work on all of the trout species and my field experience has shown that there is hardly any color preference between rainbows, browns, cutthroats, brooks or any other landlocked trout species.

The Beaver works well near the surface and in the depths. I like slow and short line strips in either situation. Exceptions are the fun (and exasperating) aspect of our sport and we must be ready for them! Full sinking lines make a big difference with most nymphs—this one included. I never use weight with this pattern because I like to retain that slim and sparse-body effect. In a size 16, the slimly tapered Beaver is highly reminiscent of various midges and some mayflies.

In slow meandering streams, the floating line is king. The leader should be adjusted for the width of the particular river you are fishing. In a 40-foot creek, a nine-foot, 4X or 6X is just about right to slowly sink this fur-bodied fly to the bottom. The fly must be carefully cast across and upstream. Let the gliding current take the fly to the bottom. The most drag-free method is to keep the line up in the air, but it must be held taut. Then, continue to keep the line as straight as possible as the fly continues drifting downstream.

In larger and faster rivers, I use a size 12 Beaver since the mayflies are likely to be a bit larger in such water. Any retrieve should be slight and brief since the most important thing is the cross-current drift. One must make a dead-drift, move up current, make a new cast, and follow with another drift of the fly.

The Beaver is also effective in a size 20, but this is for either a surface technique (much like dry fly fishing) or at depths of up to three or four feet in a pond or lake. Inching the fly along the bottom of a shallow reservoir can be murder on a hungry trout. The bottom technique is effective during sparse mayfly hatches, or when nothing is happening. If the trout are rather small, it's better to look for deeper holes and to fish with a larger pattern.

One needs rising trout in order to use the surface method. Cast to a riser fishing a size 16 or 20 Beaver like a dry fly. A slight pull wiggles it to the surface, from the film, and often tantalizes a nearby trout. Cast well upstream of the feeding trout for the second method, but remember that the distance of the cast will vary with the intensity of the feeding and the clarity of the water. A four-foot cast will be fine during a "super-hatch" or in muddy water, while at least eight or more feet is needed when a five-foot bottom is able to be seen clearly, or if the trout are feeding rather sporadically from one type of insect to another. (Both of these methods work well in lakes and streams.)

Black Midge Pupa

Body: Slender dubbing of fur
Rib: Fine wire or thread
Head: Slight balling of fur dubbing

I have picked the Black Midge Pupa because it is the most common shade for both the wing and pupa throughout most of the United States. On certain Sierra Nevada lakes though, the blood or red Midge is more common and there are certainly plenty of brown and gray hatches which bedevil us fly fishers from Pennsylvania, New Mexico, Arizona, California, Colorado and Oregon, where I have personally toured and fished. Still, the black species predominates. Two factors which make the coloration vary are the season of the year, and the time of day. Most gray-colored midges I've seen have been hovering above the waterline late on summer afternoons, while the blood or red ones have been active during that strange time between spring and summer.

However, all midge pupae fish much the same way. The worst problem when writing about midge pupae though is that there are too many tying styles. Kaufmann's catalog shows five: the Swannundaze, the Suspender, the Serendipity, the Chironomid Pupa and the Palomino. I prefer the sparsely dubbed body which Hafle and Hughes use in *The Complete Book of Western Hatches,* called the Traditional Midge Pupa.

Despite the differences between Eastern and Western tying styles for midge pupae, there are two basic ways to fish it—on the surface or along the bottom. Most of us think of midging trout when we think of midges and that is a great place to begin too.

The two main ingredients necessary are: a hatch of those black or gray little devils and rising trout. The idea is simple, but doing it is maddening because it becomes excruciatingly difficult to pull off when the size of the rising trout are enough to make one sweat.

With the pupa on a 6X tippet, cast it whisper-light, just inches short of a trout's snout, let it rest one second, then barely twitch it. A second twitch is almost too much. Keep an eye on the pod of rising trout. Quietly, lift the line and cast toward another riser, breathe deeply, and hope for the best. My first trout caught on a midge pupa was no monster—yet the two-pound rainbow did a lot for my ego.

(Those were the days when 6X tippets tested at one pound. If I could find some again, I'd use it. It really seems to fish better.)

With a size 16 or 18 Black Midge Pupa knotted on a 4X, 10-foot leader and a sinking line, plumb the bottom near a known trout lair, or weed bed, and fish it dead-slow. Down deep, the leader needs to be a bit stronger for the jolt of the strike and to keep trout from becoming tangled in weeds or stumps.

I have never noticed any bad hinge effect with a small fly on a slightly heavier tippet. Begin with a slow sinking line. (Use a faster one only if necessary.) The ideal method would be to use a floating line and a leader almost three times longer than the depth one desires to fish. It is an English method which Brian Clarke describes very well in his book, *The Pursuit of Stillwater Trout.*

The history of the midge dates back to Cotton's time but the many differences in its fly tying styles have been created during the last 20 to 30 years.

Pheasant Tail

Tail: 2-3 Pheasant tail fibers
Body: 3-5 Pheasant tail fibers wound with copper wire
Hackle: Brown

Whenever the Gold Ribbed Hare's Ear doesn't have its usual magic, the Pheasant Tail seems to work better—but near the surface of a lake.

I am thinking now of several occasions when I couldn't even interest a bluegill while another tuber netted several rainbows close to two pounds in short order. I worked towards the fisherman out in the middle of the lake. I was using a Wet Cel II with a Gold Ribbed Hare's Ear. He kept telling me that he was fishing near the surface with a size 12 Pheasant Tail. In a moment, I was doing the same thing with my second rod. (This, of course, is when I am supposed to say that I netted a half dozen four pounders in the next 20 minutes but that was not the case. In fact, I didn't hook even one but I carefully remembered the advice!)

We were the only two tubers working the middle of the lake during a midsummer wind. Trout react to those warm breezes and sometimes come to the surface, but they usually cruise closer to shoreline weeds at such a time. That day, on a small Sierra Nevada trout lake, was truly a freak. It was the first, and only time, I found a few trout mindlessly wandering about "miles" away from any kind of cover.

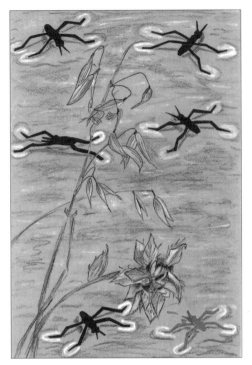

Under similar conditions, I would head to food shelves, use a floating line with a nine to 10-foot leader, tie on a size 16 Pheasant Tail, and jerk it quickly, and parallel, to the weed- or stump-covered food shelves. Try to do these two actions at once: jerking the fly near the surface, while being parallel with the shoreline at distances between 15 to 50 feet. (The latter depends upon the point at which the shelf suddenly drops to a depth that a 10-foot leader cannot reach.)

A somewhat brighter pattern than the Gold Ribbed Hare's Ear, the Pheasant Tail works better when the water is choppy or murky. Of course, there are some mayfly drake nymphs it looks like. Yet, near the bottom, the Gold Ribbed Hare's Ear works much better in my opinion.

In a river, the Pheasant Tail appears to work better than the Gold Ribbed Hare's Ear in quiet spots like pools, backwaters and in currents which slowly, and evenly, glide down a meadow slope. An upstream, cross-current cast takes an unweighted fly close to the bottom—if the leader is long enough.

I think this pattern is best fished unadorned of bead heads, split shot and a weighted body. It might be because the fiery-brown body resembles mayfly nymphs which are slender in shape. Most strikes seem to occur on the retrieve, when the fly reaches a mid-depth level which makes me think that the trout have ascending nymphs on their minds.

At any rate, the Pheasant Tail works best near the surface and not much deeper than six feet.

The bead head version of this fly is rather popular, but I also know that most fly anglers strip flies much faster than I do. While I fish a Pheasant Tail as a slow-moving bug or nymph, some of you are apparently fishing the bead head version more like a streamer. In fact, such a nymph looks more like a small fish or tadpole to me but it's all a moot point as long as we catch the fish which lunge out and pulsate our hearts!

Kaufmann's Stone (Brown)

Body: Mixed: 50% Brown and
50% Claret, amber, orange, rust, black,
Rib: Brown swannundaze
Wings: Dark turkey clipped
Tail: Brown goose fiber

Ted Trueblood was one of the first to undertake a study of Western fly fishing and tying styles. He became known for his two-tone brown and yellow nymph. It was soon dubbed Ted's Stonefly. The Montana Nymph, the other two-tone chenille pattern, is black and orange. At some point, this pattern evolved into the Bitch Creek when someone added the white feelers at each end of the hook and wound hackle near the eye.

From Schwiebert to Kaufmann, the stonefly nymph has evolved into the highly imitative forms which have dominated waters since the mid-1980s—and Kaufmann's pattern is, at the least, one of the most popular. It is available in black, gold, brown, and tan—four common shades of the natural nymph.

(I have to admit I like the older and more suggestive patterns better. Their very suggestiveness makes them adaptable to many fly fishing situations—from bass lakes to pasture rivers. It's important to remember that most stonefly nymphs are found in fast, tumbling currents where a fly does not usually have to be highly imitative.)

The Kaufmann pattern is among the best if you want an exact imitation, while Ted's Stonefly or the Montana Nymph is fine for an angler like me.

In any case, any stonefly nymph is best fished in fast and rocky currents. The real nymphs are weak swimmers or clamberers. To imitate their behavior, it is best to make a cross-current cast and dead-drift the fly through the currents. To get it on the bottom, the nymph must be weighted and fished with a fast sinking Wet Tip. I like to do other things too, like plummet a size 12 Ted's Stonefly to the bottom of a slow pool and slowly jerk it a bit towards me. This method requires a four- or five-foot leader on either a Wet Tip or a full sinking line. The Wet Tip requires a cross-stream drift while the full sinking line can be cast straight downstream. This is an early spring tactic, for late April or May, just after the worst runoff.

Stonefly nymphs are pretty much useless in a trout lake—at least for me.

A large food item, these flies are worth having ranging from a size 4 to a size 12, but sizes 8 and 6 are a decent compromise if money is tight. Brown and black are probably the two most common shades but it is wise to add the gold pattern since it is a common shade for stonefly nymphs in many of the Rocky Mountain streams.

American March Brown (Nymph)

Body: Brown floss
Wing Case: Natural gray duck quill
Tail: Dark moose fibers
Rib: Stripped peacock herl
Thorax: Peacock herl
Hackle: Brown hackle, wrapped over thorax

This was one of the biggest mysteries that I discovered during my research for this book. Neither the American March Brown (nymph) nor the March Brown (nymph) could be found in Orvis, Kaufmann's, or Fly Shop catalogs—yet they are basic nymph patterns for any fly angler. Maybe, because of the sudden emphasis on lakes and streams of the Rocky Mountains, its history as an Eastern pattern shuffled the March Brown (nymph) to a dark corner but that is a very big mistake. It is the only pattern in this book which might be hard to find.

We all know that there are a lot of brown mayfly nymphs, scuds, beetles and larva floating around. For that reason, the American March Brown, from a size 14 to a size 20, is among the very best for limestone or spring creeks. A size 20 nymph can be fished in the surface film on a dead-drift being cast upstream, ahead of the trout, or where a trout ought to be. Mend the line to give the fly a drag-free drift. It seems to work best not to give the fly any action.

In stillwaters, I work the nymph right on the bottom. I have discovered a way to fish it rather slowly in order to imitate snails down there. (I give the grimy details in my book *Advanced Lake Fly Fishing: The Skillful Tuber.*) The main thing is to strip the fly back towards the tube as slowly as possible. If it makes you yawn, the fly is being fished correctly.

The American March Brown works in most rivers or lakes. The pattern has brought me a lot of rainbows measuring up to four pounds. I use it mainly in a size 12. For midget mayflies, a size 20 is much better.

The American March Brown has a long history. Throughout the years, there have been various dressings for it. James Chetham's 1861 dressing was referred to as the "Moorish Brown" yet the pattern can also be traced back to Charles Cotton. Many of the world's greatest tiers (such as Alfred Ronalds, George Bainbridge and probably Hewitt), had their own ideas on how the fly ought to be tied.

Scud

Tail: Hackle fibers to match body color
Body: Gray, tan or olive sparkle Orlon yarn or dubbing blend
Shell back: Colored or clear plastic
Rib: Clear monofilament
Antennae: Hackle fiber to match body color

This version was created to imitate scuds when they gather together in deep sections of weedy food shelves in lakes and reservoirs. Usually, it is best fished with some weight, a long leader and a floating line. The retrieve should be intermixed with sharp jerks and pauses. A Wet Tip helps to reach depths past five feet unless you don't mind using a 15-foot leader. With the extra-long leader, the timing of the cast must be slowed down a bit. One mistake could be disastrous! It is not a method for breezes though—let alone a strong wind.

In a lake, any time I have used the Scud as a searching pattern, it has scored a big fat goose egg—but I plummeted the depths with a full sinking line. My best advice it to use this pattern when the "real thing" shows itself in the weed beds.

In a scud-filled spring creek, this pattern will work well anytime. It should be cast upstream and drifted through currents. Add an occasional light line strip to dart the fly, but it must be bumped along the bottom for successful results.

One last note for fly tiers—the scud swims in the water with its back straight so there is no need for the curved hook. The back is arched only when the scud rests.

They can be tan, olive, pink or orange but I think, the first two are the most widely dispersed throughout the West. They are available in sizes 10 through 18, but sizes 14 and 16 are likely to be your best choices.

It is too recent a pattern to have a history.

Prince (Nymph)

Body: Peacock herl
Tail: Brown stripped goose quill
Wing: White stripped goose
Rib: Fine flat gold tinsel
Hackle: Brown hackle

If there is an "attractor" nymph, this is the one—at least for me. The white wing almost makes the pattern look like a streamer and that should be a clue on how to fish it.

I had been intrigued by its look for some time before I finally bought a few. My inclination was to retrieve it dead-slow on the bottom. The results were not the kind that I wanted.

Then, an intuitive moment had me knot a size 12 Prince onto my 4X tippet. I fished it deep along a food shelf lined with weeds sprouting up from five foot depths. The shiny sides of rainbow trout had been carefully eluding my usual dark- and dull-colored nymphs. The factor going against me (and other fly anglers who had left for deeper water by the dam) was the ultra-clear water. I, half on purpose, let the Prince snag on a weed and then I sharply pulled it loose. In the same moment, a rainbow lunged for it and I struck. The result was the loud pop of my leader. I swear that trout looked up and snickered at me as I glumly sat in my tube. At least I learned something—fish the Prince as if it were a streamer. After I fixed and lengthened the leader, subsequent casts were more carefully presented and I landed some hefty rainbows. (I had better not try a weight or length estimation since this event was long ago and we all know what memory does to an angler!)

The shallow water method, with a floating line and long leader (about 10 feet), will work best with this pattern. With two light strips of lead under the body, the Prince will quickly reaches five-foot depths. Quickly strip the fly when it reaches the bottom and then begin a retrieve which matches the two-step beat of a march. One will be able to observe the pattern in clear water. (Such a retrieve is relief from the slow one I use to probe the mid-lake depths. Out there, the same two-step strip does little good.)

My theory is that the faster and larger water creatures stay in the top eight feet while the smaller and slower ones stay near the bottom. In any case, the two-beat retrieve works the best for this pattern which I use exclusively in a size 12. I used to think that a size 10 or an eight would be better in large reservoirs which hold all sorts of game fish but I have proven myself wrong too many times.

The Prince worked well in fast tumbling rivers when I drifted it downstream with natural currents. With a bead head Prince Nymph, a bottom bouncing retrieve works well—at least that is what I am told. With a floating line or Wet Tip, the fly can be "jigged." It ought to work but I have yet to try it.

Much of my work with the Prince Nymph is still under study. Let me know if you have a better way to fish it, okay?

Streamers and Bucktails

Woolly Bugger

Tail: A bunch of marabou fibers of matching color
Body: Chenille; black, brown, olive
Hackle: Of matching color

It took me forever to decide which streamer should begin this section. The differences between many of these patterns, too often, are quite slight. My biggest hurdle was between the Woolly Bugger and the Muddler Minnow, but then there was the Marabou Leech and Matuka Bucktail!

I finally decided that I use the Woolly Bugger the most frequently so here we are! One should never be without: all-brown, all-black, and all-olive Buggers. (I also carry many of the two-toned patterns but these are my "big" three.)

There is hardly a method that will not work. In this section though, I will describe those which seem to be the very best during spring, summer and fall, on one given mountain lake at about 5,700 feet. A reservoir at this altitude, will have healthy weed beds which will provide forage food so that trout will grow quickly and become fat.

Generally speaking, ice and freezing temperatures will be gone by April. At this time, the days may be bright but the trout will still hover close to the bottom. With a sinking line, slowly and evenly strip a black Woolly Bugger (in a size 10 or a size 12) along the bottom. Try to visualize the hackles barely wavering in the water. Start out in the middle of the water, yet near a food shelf. Make the casts parallel to the shelf and then toward it. Slowly work inward but keep the bucktail in depths of 10 feet or more. (In a boat, one could use a depth finder but it really isn't necessary.)

Stream anglers should seek quiet spots near banks or quiet holes at this time of year. Inch the same Bugger along the bottom as well. A bit of lead may be helpful to keep it down below.

Typical May weather means that trout are beginning to feed. Probe the eight to 15-foot depths of lakes with a size 12 black or brown Bugger and work it slowly along the bottom. For variety, you could tie on a size 8 bucktail of the same shade and retrieve it along the bottom in fast and erratic strips. One of these two methods will usually bring results. (Olive is a prime shade toward the end of the month and into June.)

In late June, trout will move into the shallows. At that time, a jerky and quick retrieve often works, but keep the fly on the bottom. Even the time of day can make a difference. I recommend that you drag a stream thermometer through the water with a loop-less stringer. Always be on the search for the prime feeding water temperatures of 58 to 64 degrees F. (When warmer weather eventually predominates, I suggest using a brown-colored Bugger to do the trick.)

Small rivers (under 60 feet in width) need a size 10 or a size 12 Bugger. A brown-colored one is likely to be best in early summer months. With a floating line and bead head Bugger, let the fast currents take the bucktail to the bottom and then jig it upstream toward where you are standing.

Big, tumbling rivers require a Wet Tip, four-foot leader and sometimes some lead under the body of the fly. A black or brown Bugger, in a size 8 or 10, can either be dead-drifted like a nymph in the current, or stripped erratically across and upstream. Better yet, combine those two tactics!

From the end of June and on into July, it is time to go back to the fishing holes found in big rivers and lakes. Remember to crawl a size 12, all-black Bugger slowly along the bottom of a lake but don't forget that when a greenish tint takes over the surface in mid-July or early August, it is time to head for alpine lakes located above 10,000 feet or to your favorite river. When on the river, river fishermen will need to concentrate on holes or deep runs and crawl the same Bugger slowly along the bottom. (Yet, I still often choose to slug things out on that lower reservoir by probing its depths with an olive or black Bugger in a size 12.)

The very best summer tactic is to fish at dawn, or where legal, at night. But, as for fishing, I prefer the daylight.

Summer trout streamer fishing—anywhere—usually means slower and slower strips with a black or brown Woolly Bugger. Most of the time, I prefer to use a size 12. (There is a point in October though when the temperatures sharply plummet and the trout can go crazy—along with some the fly fishermen!)

The most important thing about fall trout streamer fishing is choice. Carefully choose the lake or river best known for large rainbows or browns, and concentrate your efforts on those stretches of shoreline known to hold such trout. In these known trout sections, cast towards stumps and weed beds with the biggest streamer you carry. Brown over yellow, or black over brown Buggers, I think, work the best.

I recommend that you use at least a 7 weight outfit with a 2X tippet because long, fast, furious strips elicit arm-jolting strikes from trophy-sized trout. This must be the keenest time of concentration and anticipation.

Here in California, I can fish foothill and valley lakes during the winter. During sunny, 50 degree F. days in December or February, I choose to fish either an all-black or a black and gray Bugger. I fish it on the bottom with a sleepy and slow retrieve.

The Woolly Bugger evolved from the Woolly Worm sometime during the 1980s. It has not had much of a chance to form a history—but it most certainly will. Although the pattern works virtually anywhere, most of its fame comes from the West or the West Coast.

Muddler Minnow

Tail: Mottled turkey quill
Body: Gold tinsel
Under Wing: Gray squirrel tail
Wing: Mottled turkey quill
Color: Deer hair, spun
Head: Deer hair, spun and clipped

The Muddler Minnow could possibly be the only pattern which needs to be fished differently depending upon its size. A size 6 is, more or less, in the middle of the range. Each smaller pattern, down to a size 12, needs to be retrieved slower and slower—eventually to a crawl. And of course the opposite is true when going up to a size 2/0.

My theory is that the smaller Muddler Minnows look the most like bugs while the biggest ones take on the appearance of forage fish, crustaceans or even small frogs or mice! (The Muddler's floating abilities make that seem possible to me.)

Here's one possible way to use the Muddler Minnow in midsummer. The air feels like a million degrees and the surface layer of the lake has more than just a green tint to it. Most anglers bypass such lakes, and I don't blame them, but by being persistent (or stubborn), I make attempts to learn things and sometimes I do.

With a size 12 Muddler Minnow on such a lake, I head for its deepest hole and crawl the fly so slowly that I almost put myself to sleep—until a fat brown or rainbow takes the fly and heads for the distant shoreline! Do not expect these results right away though. It does take time and a lot of persistence to find deep water trout. When you do, mark the spot with a mental or written note. (Remember that deep holes in any impoundment will produce throughout the year regardless of the weather or water conditions.)

Always be sure that the fly ticks the bottom. Between worrying about losing a few patterns and netting a six-pound trout, I always choose the latter. (My first trout that weighted close to two pounds was caught in this fashion and I will never forget it!)

In a small river with riffles, runs and pools, tie on a size 10 Muddler and cast it across the currents. With enough weight on it to tick the upper sides of sunken rocks, let it drift downstream and across the lanes of current. Strip only enough off to keep tension on the line. Zip the fly straight up the current and start all over again. (With this method, the fly may look like a mad tom or even a crayfish.)

The same idea works with a size 8 or 6 Muddler fished in a river which has the width of at least 60 feet. Here, a fast sinking Wet Tip and a short four-foot leader may work better than lead. If nothing else, it will cast better.

Muddlers up until the 0 sizes are for rivers which span out to 100 feet or more. Most of these rivers are the Rocky Mountain or Northwest "lunker" trout hot spots. With cross-stream swings and fast erratic strips, the Muddler will probably look like a small fish, a large crayfish, or a small creature trying to hurry toward land.

In deep runs and pools, a fast sinking line and a weighted fly will usually work best. A bead head Muddler should probably be fished quickly and in darts. I prefer the original pattern though.

A size 2 unweighted Muddler fished in minnow-like retrieves over the tops of weedy shorelines in big rivers or lakes is likely to rouse a lunker from its kitchen or den—especially when big browns cruise the shallows and become interested in love.

The Muddler Minnow also fishes well on the surface but now we challenge the dry fly expert. A size 8 Muddler dead-drifted in currents could resemble a grasshopper. In the average stream where most of us fish, I would use a size 10 or a size 12 and pull it under the surface as I moved it toward me. It could be a small land creature or a dying minnow. In any case, I know it works!

Don Gapen originated the Muddler Minnow when he needed to imitate the Cockatush minnow which he found in Ontario, Canada's Nipigon River. It is a flat headed minnow which lives under rocks. In some regions of Wisconsin, they were called Muddlers, thus the name.

Dan Bailey is most likely the first tier to incorporate marabou into the pattern.

Honestly, there is not a fish which wouldn't go for at least one size or style of this fly.

Marabou Leech

Tail: Small clump of black or brown marabou
Body: Slim chenille of same color
Wing: Black or brown marabou tied in small clumps
along length of body

This is the style of the original bucktail: a tail, body, and marabou wing. It is a very simple and neatly formed bucktail which is pure murder when fished correctly. The full-winged bucktail, which covers all sides of the hook, is specialized for lunker-hunting or fishing at night. The same is true for the Spuddlers. I think the original bucktail is the best for all-around lake and stream fishing. All-black is the most standard shade for this pattern.

It became popular in the limestone country of Pennsylvania

where the streams often have a yellowish tint. It was particularly true in one river which had currents that stained the breeches of Civil War soldiers. Its name is reflective of this history—the Yellow Breeches Creek! When I lived in that snowy state, it became one of my favorite rivers. There, I learned two ways to fish the Marabou Leech.

The method I used most often was simple. I would cast a size 12 Marabou Leech cross-stream and follow its drift with the tip of my rod until the pattern was directly below me. Momentarily, I'd let the Marabou Leech hang in the current before I would give it a slight dart up and into the current. I sometimes let it rest a second time before I inched it back towards me. About midway through the retrieve, I'd sidle downstream a few steps, lift the floating line, and cast across the current once again. (This searching method is best when exploring and learning the terrain of a river.)

A bit of lead under the body is needed to get the fly below four-foot depths. This is important because big trout like to hug the bottom and its cover. I would not add a bead eye to this pattern though. When trout are in deep spots where sunken timber, weeds, or rocks are located, the Marabou Leech can then be directed down the current to that spot.

This idea takes us to the second method. It was no good for me, but it worked well for Ed Koch before he began his study of terrestrials. It is easy, but takes great patience. The same size 12 black Marabou Leech is drifted downstream and then directly in front of a trout's hideout near the bank. (Clear water will help you see the fly.) Waver the marabou feathers back and forth in the current until either the trout goes for it or you can't stand it anymore!

In a deep pool, where the bottom cannot be observed, another technique is possible. Weight an unweighted Marabou Leech with a large split shot right at, or on, the head of the hook and jig it up and down on the bottom. (A sneakier approach is simply to let line out and let the fly drift down into the placid currents and then down to the bottom.) Bring the fly back upstream by jerking the rod tip up and down. Keep the line taut by stripping in line only when necessary. If that becomes tiresome, one can also cast the same floating line, nine-foot leader and the weighted Bucktail Leech across the current and then bring it back in jig-like fashion across the pool or straight upstream.

At the opposite end of the spectrum, a size 12 Marabou Leech in white can be fished like a wet fly or nymph in the mid-currents of a riffle.

The same pattern on a standard size 10 hook can be presented in the film to a rising trout. This is a technique I have observed. It takes a quiet approach and a careful aim in order to lightly drop the fly about four feet or so ahead of a feeding brown or rainbow. The line should be stripped out just enough to flutter the feathers directly in front of the trout's eyes. Like I said, I know it works because I saw it happen. The soft-spoken angler did everything perfectly.

In a lake, I shine much better. With a Wet Cel II sinking line, I can reach depths of about 25 feet. I usually begin with a black Marabou Leech but brown and white also work well. (The latter, I think, is more effective in midsummer.)

Out in the middle of a lake and towards the bottom, slow and short strips, no longer than two-inches, can prove successful—even when bait fishermen on the bank are having a terrible day! There are other times too though when a medium to fast retrieve wakes up a sleeping trout or attracts cruising ones near shoreline weeds.

I use the all-olive pattern when the others don't work or where a lot of weeds and moss dominate. It can be fished on a sinking line or with a floating line. The idea is to fish either just over the bottom moss, or in the pockets between the weeds near the bank. Short, fast strips work well on the bottom as well as near the surface.

I fish the size 8 Marabou Leech in big, deep, rocky reservoirs but often go down to a size 12 in small and weedy ones.

When wading large Rocky Mountain rivers, I would fish with a size 6 until someone proved to me that I needed a larger one. Size 4 and larger Marabou Bucktails, in my opinion, are "lunker" flies. These larger flies cast much easier on 8 or 9 weight fly rods. Such equipment is for trophy trout, salmon, steelhead and ocean fish. Most of us are perfectly fine with 5 to 7 weight rods. Joe Brooks was among the first to fish with Marabou Bucktails. He has written about them in several books, such as *The Complete Book of Fly Fishing*. He describes how to fish with both the simple black Marabou and its variations. Dan Bailey was among the first to make the Bucktail fuller and brighter.

Matuka

Tail: Brown or black fibers of hackle
Body: Brown or black chenille
Ribbing: Silver tinsel

The brown and black Matuka patterns seem to be the most effective. The brown pattern is imitative of a minnow scurrying along a bank side weed bed when it is stripped in fast and erratic strips. As a searching pattern on the bottom of a lake, I like to strip it in short and then long strips, in one retrieve, as the fly scurries from one type of cover to another. With this pattern, I prefer to use a floating line and a long leader. Its length will depend on how deep I fish the fly. It may not make sense but the brown Matuka does not seem very effective near rocks or rocky cliffs. It works best near weeds and logs.

The black Matuka does better, in my opinion, between five and ten feet. To fish those depths effectively, I first tried a Wet Tip but I found that I didn't like them. I lost my "direct feel" to the fly with that hybrid line. A short cast with the Wet Cel II worked fine. (Years later, I finally purchased another spool for a Wet Cel I which let me enjoy a longer retrieve.) Near the bottom, I dart a size 8 or a size 12 black Matuka in about three-inch pulls. The size of the fly depends upon the season, game fish available, and lake size. Early in the year, and in the midst of the hot season, the smaller size is definitely better even if big trout are around. The larger size is more consistent in the lower foothill reservoirs where almost any freshwater fish can be found.

In currents, the Matuka catches a lot of trout with a typical cross-stream cast and upstream mend, but once again, stick with smaller sizes. It really is amazing how many trout weighing close to four pounds will hit them. (One must not want to deal with trout less than 16 inches if they use bucktails or streamers larger then a size 8.) At the end of the drift, the fly should be stripped directly upstream or across a lane of currents. I am amused when anglers pick the line up immediately at the end of the drift and quickly start over again as they quickly move to another spot. This method covers a lot of water quickly, but it also misses trout in hidden pockets.

The length of the leader, cast, and retrieve is dictated by the width of the creek. A small stream artist can make the best use of this pattern in those riffling currents edging against a line of tangled roots and timber. A fast, upstream retrieve with a brown Matuka, close to a similar edge is likely to bring a savage strike from a big trout.

The Matuka originated in New Zealand but the state of California was where the fly was first fished in the United States. For a complete listing of pattern and color combinations, look for a copy of Keith Draper's *Trout Flies of New Zealand*.

When Joseph D. Bates Jr., one of the most acclaimed of streamer experts, visited Melbourne in 1964, Major Theodore Brun gave him a complete set of Matuka dressings. Perhaps, Bates was one of the first to fish the pattern in the states.

Light Spruce

Head: Black
Tail: Peacock sword fibers
Body: Red woolly mixed with peacock herl

Mainly found in three sizes—6, 8 and 10—the Spruce Streamer is one of the best candidates for a minnow imitation. For that reason, it is best fished in the shallows and retrieved in fairly fast and short line strips. Quite possibly, the very best method is to hurry it over the tops of weed beds with fairly short and fast jerks.

In moving currents, the cross-stream drift with short and sharp jerks (which imitate a wounded minnow) usually work well—but it

Nymphs

Gold Ribbed Hare's Ear

Gray Nymph

Zug Bug

Beaver

Black Midge Pupag

Pheasant Tail

Kaufmann's Stone

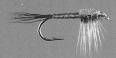

American March
Brown (Nymph)

Scud

Prince Nymph

All flies tied by Dale "Lobo" Barton
Photographed by Jim Schollmeyer

Plate I

Streamers and Bucktails

Woolly bugger

Muddler Minnow

Marabou Bucktail (Leech)

Matuka

Light Spruce

Zonker

Sheep Shad

Allies Chenille Coachman

Black Nosed Dace

Mickey Finn

Plate II

Wets

Brown Hackle Peacock

Gray Hackle Yellow

"True" Woolly Worm

Brown Woolly Worm

Black Woolly Worm

Gray-brown Woolly Worm

Olive Woolly Worm

Hare's Ear

Black Ant

Coachman

Plate III

Dries

Adams

Light Cahill

Dark Cahill

Bivisible

Irresistible

Hairwing Royal Coachman

Elk-Hair Caddis

Dave's Hopper

Black Ant

Black Midge

Plate IV

works best fished rather purposefully near known weeds or timber rather than cast hither and yonder without a particular plan. One could probably settle for the Spruce Streamer in a size 8. I much prefer this size in moving currents.

The Light Spruce is one of the most prominent Northwestern patterns and is an innovation of the Improved Governor pattern which is named after long deceased Godfrey of Seaside, Oregon. Originally, it was tied to take summer and fall runs of cutthroat trout sometimes referred to as "blueback" trout.

One variation of the Light Spruce is the Spruce Bucktail which is tied with badger hair instead of badger hackle wing.

The Silver Spruce variation, first tied by Polly Rosoborough at Al Kellogg's suggestion, is tied with a small bunch of badger hair. It used to be very popular on Oregon's Nehalem, Trask, and Nestucca rivers.

Another variation, the Red Spruce, is tied with a red woolly body and ribbed with silver tinsel.

Zonker

Body: Mylar tubing (usually weighted)
Wing: Natural gray tan stripped rabbit fur
Tail: Unraveled silver tubing
Hackle: Grizzly hen hackle

There are silver, purple, black, and olive Zonkers. These patterns are intended for big fish patterns since they range from a size 2 to an 8. The largest should be used on a 7 weight outfit but an 8 or 9 weight would be better.

Weedy places like Henry's Fork Lake are made-to-order for the olive Zonker. Casting to the weeds and hurrying the streamer back in six-to 10-inch strips usually works best, but be prepared for savage strikes! This definitely is not delicate work! A leader need not be over 7 and 1/2 feet and tippets ought to be 1X, or even 0X.

In big and fast rivers, make long cross-stream casts and drifts with a fast sinking Wet Tip and weighted black or purple pattern. The most important thing is to get the streamer to the bottom. Strips should be short and quick. Areas with rocks and timber usually attract the biggest trout so search there. Otherwise, use the same method for exploring along, and through, the river itself. Such streamer fishing is best either in the last few hours of the day, at night where it's legal, or from late September through October. (Be prepared for snowstorms and sore wrists!)

Two other ways to fish the Zonker successfully are by float-tube trolling (after a rainstorm), or when trout are slashing through schools of minnow or shad. In the latter case, the silver pattern is likely to be the best.

Olive may be the best in stillwaters while black is probably the best universally. Purple, on any fly, has never done much for me. I suspect it is better in currents, or for anadromous salmonids.

The best overall size is likely to be a 6. As far as color is concerned, I would choose black. It makes an excellent bead head streamer as well but I would stick with the original.

The pattern was originated by Dan Byford of Steamboat Springs, Colorado.

Sheep Shad

Underwing: White Icelandic sheep, pearl Krystal flash
Beard: Icelandic sheep, pearl Krystal flash
Body: Gray dun saddle hackle, with wide
pearl Krystal flash on either side
Cheeks: Mallard flank feathers
Eyes: Plastic doll eyes

The Sheep Shad was tailor-made for the coastal lakes of California—in particular, for Berryessa and Folsom lakes. When shad come to the surface and cause a feeding binge of rainbows of up to six pounds, this is the primary pattern to use. Other similar patterns work, but this is the pattern most anglers recommend—usually in a size 4.

Cast it into a pod of frenzied feeding trout and strip it in long and fast jerks. A six or seven-foot, 2X leader is fine but some anglers like to go up to 0X since the trout react with brutal and hard strikes.

The Sheep Shad can also be used in large rivers for trout and shad. A cross-stream cast, downstream drift, and fast retrieve often make for a very exciting day. Be prepared for sore shoulder and arm muscles.

Allies Chenille Coachman

Tail: Red hackle fibers or red dyed bucktail
Rib: Fine copper wire
Body: 1/4 olive chenille, 1/2 red floss, 1/4 olive chenille
Hackle: Brown saddle hackle, tied folded to extend to point of hook
Wing: White calftail

Overall, coachman patterns may very well be the best of the bright and fancy patterns.

In a size 10, this is an excellent exploring pattern for a small stream angler. With short upstream casts, and gentle but fast cross-current retrieves, one can quickly find where the rainbow or brook trout lay. It is done just right when the fly is a bit faster than the current because this particular action will flutter the hair wing. These must be quiet presentations which avoid line shadows and splashes. A 5 weight DT line and a seven-foot 4X tippet will help.

With a fly one size larger and with some weight at the eye of the hook, the same presentation works in larger rivers. A bead head Coachman strikes me as a great river pattern.

My countless hours and days with any hair wing coachman on a lake were 100% worthless save for one dumb bluegill hitting one of the very few white coachmans I tied. (It might have been the only fish caught by anything that came out of my vise half a million years ago!)

The coachman's development (and history) developed from the wet fly of that same name which goes back to the days of Cotton and Walton.

Black Nose Dace

Tail: Short tuft of bright red yarn
Body: Silver tinsel
Wing: White, then black, then brown bucktail
(each slightly longer than other)
Head: Black

One problem when picking a group of "best" patterns is the divergence of thought between Eastern and Western styles and types. With wet flies and nymphs, many such differences are dissolving but that is much less true with bucktails or streamers.

I almost put the "Rainbow Trout" pattern in this spot but I was thinking of the streamer, not the mylar pattern found in the Kaufmann's catalog. These flashy patterns catch a lot of river trout but I had in mind more imitative patterns: the Silver Minnow or Black Nose Dace. The Dace pattern is general and looks like almost any little fish which swims in an Eastern brook or a big churning Western river. I do not like it with a bead head but try it if the idea strikes your fancy.

My first three years of steady lake fly fishing shouted loud and clear that a hair wing type streamer is worthless in stillwaters. Thinking back on it now, I realize such fly fishing was exploratory. If trout are actively chasing fingerlings or minnows, a quickly darted size 10 Black Nose Dace would work well. During a summer windstorm, trout often come in toward the shoreline. The bright mylar Black Nose Dace, at this time, might grab the attention of a wandering trout, but Kaufmann's only sells it in a size 4! Such a big fly in wind is a very lethal weapon! The same pattern, in a size 10, ought to be good for a windy lake situation though.

This, and any hair wing streamer, is made-to-order for moving currents. The best fly action will be imparted by the riffles and runs rather than the angler. Both Kaufmann's pattern, and any other Black Nose Dace, would be fished the same way in rivers—across and downstream.

Let the fly work down and then deep into the current. Across divergent speeds of currents, a long leader with weight near the fly and floating line are usually the best. Typically, at the end of the drift, the fly is jerked straight back upstream, but I'm beginning to suspect intermittent strips and pauses across the current might be more successful. In order to do this, one must either follow the drift by sidling downstream at the same speed as the drifting fly, or by casting the fly upstream and letting it drift to the bottom somewhere straight ahead of you. In a riffle or slow run, wading along with it is reasonable but any fast current can make this tactic dangerous. A big Western stream filled with rocks will teach you that lesson very quickly!

Overall, it probably is better to use the first method. Remember though that in either case, the fly must reach the bottom since that is where the trout are usually hanging. Nine to 10 feet of leader and a weighted fly, in most cases, will do the job with successful results. The most successful fishermen will be those who do not explore but drift the fly into a known hole or where they know a stump, rock, or other such trout holding objects are.

The Black Nose Dace was originated by Art Flick of Westkill, New York to imitate a bait fish of that name. It is described in his book *Streamside Guide to Naturals and their Imitations.*

Harold Gibbs took it to the brine in his pursuit of striped bass.

Mickey Finn

Body: Silver tinsel
Ribbing: Silver oval tinsel
Wing: Yellow, red and yellow bucktail (over each other)
Head: Black

The concern for differences, between Eastern and Western fly fishermen, applies to this pattern as it did to the Black Nose Dace.

But here, there is at least one other method which is an applicable way to fish this pattern.

This bright streamer works rather well on a bright summer day or where bluegill accompany trout. (There are few lakes under 6,000 feet which are pure trout waters.)

On a bright sunny day, after too many fly changes, tie on a size 10 Mickey Finn and head for a riffle with enough depth to hold trout during the day. With an across and slightly upstream cast, let it sink a moment and then quickly bring it back toward you, but don't make too many casts to the same spot. (Just one sloppy presentation will scare the trout to the next state!)

In a lake or slow spot of a river, where bright-colored bluegill are apt to hold, the same fly poked along just fast enough to move the hair wing works well too. It's not as consistent a method as the first but nevertheless it does work.

(Can I make one gripe? The Black Nosed Dace and the Mickey Finn seem to always be tied on 6XL hooks and I don't know why. Since I began lake fly fishing, I have made many experiments with these patterns tied on 3XL and 6XL hooks. I finally determined that most of the time, nearly 100 percent of the trout are hooked on the shorter shank with few problems, while more than half of the strikes on the other shank leave me hanging with slack line. When it happened on 3XL nymphs or streamers, I dropped to Woolly Worms tied on standard sized hooks and my trouble ended.)

Summer trout are hard enough to find, and then to entice, but when they strike short and don't get hooked, one's level of sanity is tested far too much.

Give me any streamer on a 3XL hook. Larger sizes (like a size 2) might even cast better!

In 1932, a Mr. Vanderhoff introduced the Mickey Finn to author John Alden Knight who is credited for the popularity of this pattern. It was first called the Assassin but then Gregory Clark, a *Toronto Star* feature writer, re-named it the Mickey Finn since the name Assassin made him think of how Rudolph Valentino had been killed by administering too many Mickey Finns. Angling history had been made!

Wet Flies

Brown Hackle Peacock

Tail: Red floss or wool, tied short
Body: Peacock herl
Hackle: Brown
Head: Brown or black

Gray Hackle Yellow

Tail: Red floss or hackle, fibers tied short
Body: Yellow floss
Rib: Fine oval silver wire; reversed wrapped
Hackle: Grizzly hen

These two hackle wet flies almost go back to the beginning of time. Today unfortunately , they are much too underrated. I like to think of them as nymphs which is why I fish both the Brown Hackle Peacock and the Gray Hackle Yellow on the bottom—and dead slow. The main difference between these two patterns though is when I fish them.

I have found that they are not very effective much deeper than 20 feet. In a size 14 or 16, they need a long 4X tippet and a nine- or 10-foot leader attached to a Wet Cel II. The best method is to fish them just above weed beds. If necessary, use the countdown method, counting 001, 002, etc., in order to fish them just inches above a mossy or weedy bottom. (I also crawl them right on the bottom and then up, over, and through whatever debris might be there.)

This bottom fishing can be done at any time of the day—including dawn and twilight. In fact, unless I see rising trout, it is the way I fish any lake. Never assume that trout will rise just because the sun is barely cresting the earth. Sometimes, a bank angler proves me wrong but generally I will catch more, or larger fish. The second rod, rigged with floating line, is handy for the exception.

Exploratory fishing with these two patterns is highly effective. Once a productive fishing hole is located, work every corner of it by barely inching a hackle fly along the bottom. (Remember, trout move all over a lake throughout the course of a day whether for food, security or "love".) To be successful from morning until night, keep moving to every part of the lake until you know where to be, and at what different hours for each season of the year.

These hackle patterns used with a floating line, are tailor-made for trout sipping minuscule bugs or insects from just below the surface of a quiet spot in a river or lake. With a 4X, 10-foot leader, cast the fly just inches short of a feeding trout, let the fly sink just barely for a second, and then twitch it. Anything more than two twitches per trout is too much. It will make them gun-shy. Without a hit after those two light twitches, either let the fly sink to the bottom and slowly work it back toward you, or carefully pick up the floating line and cast to another feeder. (The latter would be better in a meadow river.)

I usually use this technique during most hatches and, a fair amount of time, I catch two trout while someone else is trying to decide which fly will "match the hatch". Entomology is important but, too often, particularly on a lake, a hatch can be brutally short. Pick up that second rod and cast that small wet hackle while deciphering the hatch.

A size 16 Brown Hackle Peacock will be the best pattern for early in the year, while a Gray Hackle Yellow (of the same size) would be better starting in early May. From then until summer, a Brown Hackle Brown (size 14), followed with a size 16 Yellow Hackle Gray—when the heat finally arrives—is usually about right. This is the usual progression of predominating mayflies. This also is true when bottom fishing with these hackle flies.

When the trout are not rising, (even when they are expected to early and late in the day), fish these hackle patterns in a size 14 and on the bottom of deep food shelves. There, the long leader, with a floating line, will work fine—to about five feet at the very most. Some anglers may extend their leaders to as much as 20 feet, and continue fishing with a floating line though. It requires not only perfect casting, but also a windless day which in the Rockies, the Southwest or on the West Coast, is fairly rare!

This shallow water tactic means erratic, and not quite medium strips. (I find most anglers fish too quickly.) In a lake, the cast and subsequent retrieve can be as long as you desire but in a river, it depends upon the speed of the current.

In tumbling currents, the most effective approach is across-stream and angled slightly up from your wading spot. The fly will work best dead-drifted down through one lane of the current. In the slowest and clearest water, the fly should be cast almost straight upstream. Keep the line high and tight above the surface, as the fly floats toward you. Almost any retrieve from the angler is considered too much. The idea is to fish the hackle fly like a drowned mayfly spinner, dun, or caddisfly.

I have tried to determine if different kinds of cover need different shades of flies but my results were seldom very consistent. I know that the rather old color-theory, matching trout species to various fly colors, is not very useful either.

One note for fly tiers. I have found that the Gray Hackle Yellow catches many more trout when the yellow silk body is segmented with black or brown tying thread. It looks much more like an insect. Consistently, it has out-fished the original dressing by eight to one trout a day—at the least!

Any hackle wet fly—including the two described above—pre-date most winged patterns and were the mainstay patterns when Charles Cotton and Izaak Walton fished those famed English rivers.

"True" Woolly Worm

Body: Peacock herl
Hackle: Brown, palmered over body
Head: Black (The red tail is unnecessary
and may make the fly less effective.)

My exceptional success with this pattern has mainly been in lakes, but the fly is also very effective in moving currents. In streams, with a floating line, I would free-float a size 12 pattern in riffles and runs with cross-stream casts and mends.

Recall that small flies (under a size 10 of any type) work a million times better without any weight at the eye or on the leader. If weight is added, it works best with this fly when added under the body material but it must be kept to a minimum since a thin body style works much better than a thick one.

In lakes, it is most successful when crawled along the bottom. Often, retrieves should slow down as you use smaller patterns. The reverse does not seem to apply—at least with nymphs and wet flies.

Big pools, especially sizable ones, are best thought of as a miniature pond. Send the fly to the bottom

with a long leader and work it in slow cross-stream retrieves.

The most effective "True" Woolly Worm is tied on a size 12, 3XL hook. Without the red tail, the Woolly is definitely an imitative type of fly, if it's fished correctly.

The Woolly Worm takes us back to the days of Izaak Walton and Charles Cotton. They referred to the "True" Woolly Worm as the Palmer Fly. The reason should be obvious. Originally, it was tied with a thin body of peacock herl and palmered with brown hackle. The first description of the Woolly Worm, as we know it, was in Thomas Barker's 16th century book, *The Art of Angling*.

Even after being torn apart, trout still hit the fly. I honestly cannot count the number of rainbow trout, weighing up to four pounds, that I have caught on just one of them. Even with the thread unraveling and the peacock herl torn up, the trout literally continue to attack it! The pattern is a must have.

Brown Woolly Worm

Body: Thin brown chenille
Hackle: Brown
Head: Brown

You'll discover that a size 12 Brown Woolly Worm is likely to be a best-seller. It imitates the prevalent damselfly and *Callibaetis* mayfly. Tied sparsely, trout almost smash the fly with vengeance but it must be retrieved in short and even strokes. This pattern can be fished from the bottom to the surface of a lake, since the naiad, or nymph, shoots to the top rather quickly and should be imitated with this pattern. When the upward curve of the Wet Cel II brings the fly up from the bottom debris, hurry it to the top in three- to four-inch strips. It doesn't hurt to pause and let the fly sink a moment between the fast strips though.

It's important to observe and notice things. When the naiads of the damselfly are wriggling in the film just under the surface, it's time for the floating line. My stubbornness to pick up the second rod, which holds that line, has kept me from catching many trout. I still gnash my teeth in anger knowing that I would have caught them. Unfortunately, I waited too long and the action slowed down too quickly.

Exact imitations rarely seem necessary except where anglers out-number the creatures—somewhere below all the tubes and boats—or when fishing exceptionally clear lakes. Brown, olive, green and tan represent the color progression of the damselfly naiads as the air becomes warmer and then hot. I would always try to stick with a size 12 pattern.

After the damselfly hatches have left the scene late in July, the Brown Woolly in a size 12 is still very effective when crawled over rocks, pebbles, and amidst bottom weeds, stumps and sunken debris. A size 8 Brown Woolly can be effective later in the year and near the surface. Even then, I like the fly on the sparse side and I would fish it in longer and in somewhat faster strips.

I would fish the size 12 Brown Woolly Worm during the damselfly and *Callibaetis* hatches—in rivers—the same way that I do in lakes but I might use a Wet Tip or shooting head to get the fly on the rocks. A floating line and a small split shot at the eye of the hook, will also work. In either case, the slow and easy-does-it retrieve, accompanied with an occasional fast strip to the surface, will catch most of the fish.

Spring creeks generally have intense damselfly and *Callibaetis* hatches. In these quiet waters, a floating line and long leader are almost always effective. Late in the year and after major hatches, I would drift the Brown Woolly near the bottom iof runs and holes with current. The whispery swish of the hackles is the only action needed. I would use as little lead as possible. Spring creeks, though, often demand exact imitations.

Black Woolly Worm

Body: Black
Hackle: Black
Head: Black

I like the Black Woolly Worm palmered a bit heavier than the Brown Woolly—but not much! There are at least two occasions where these two patterns produce the most trout in a lake: as a summer evening burns its way toward twilight and in April, when the water first warms to a reasonable comfort zone for trout. (I think the Black Woolly probably imitates a beetle of water bug.)

In the first situation, I tube toward the shoreline and fish in the mid-depths (eight to 15 feet). Yes, there are times when the dry fly is king at this hour but as lakes have become more crowded, big trout seem to rise less often. My theory is that trout learn from experience. They hear vibrations and notice the shadows of bank side anglers stomping their feet so they fin their way back to the depths. We anglers literally become the bogeymen of the trout world.

(Ah! But I can think of times when trout came up to the surface in the middle of a lake for a brief caddis hatch, instead of feeding at the popular time of day, when their "bogeymen" cover the surface with shadows or stomps on the ground.)

Wading anglers avoid the shadow problem but they must also keep their feet quiet both to keep from scuttling pebbles and from dirtying

the water. Bank side fly fishers must hide behind bushes and trees, while looking into the sun, walking as little as necessary and all while avoiding the edge of the lake. It's funny how we talk quietly when fishing, but these sound waves travel in the air. It's true of radios too but I go to the natural world for peace and quiet and expect to get it.

Anyway, stationed in my tube, about 50 feet or so from the bank, I cast and retrieve my size 8 Black Woolly Worm parallel to the bank. My retrieve is faster than slow but slower than a medium tempo.

Early in the year, I stick with the size 12 Black Woolly and crawl it dead-slow along the bottom. In April, more times than not, I am close to the middle of the pond or lake. It is 100 percent impossible to fish the fly too slow. At times, my persistence wanes and my head nods only to jerk it up a moment later when my line zings out with the greatest of speed.

In moving currents, I like cross-stream drifts in riffles, and upstream slow pulls in the holes. In the latter, it is most important to use a size 12 or smaller, sparsely hackled, Black Woolly. One must also avoid shadows and any unnecessary movement of the head, arms or legs. (In spring creeks, one must be even more careful of shadows and noise.)

The Black Woolly, of the same size and style, is very effective when fished upstream and artfully drifted to the bottom on a floating line with a long leader. Let the fly go through the whole drift until it is well below you. Flip the line a bit toward the middle and slowly cruise the fly back upstream. The tendency, I know, is to do a lot of casting but the trout are in the water—not the air! Fished in this fashion, the Black Woolly could look like a lot of things: a big drowned ant, stonefly, beetle or maybe even a cricket.

Gray-Brown Woolly Worm

Tail: Short red hackle fibers
Body: Gray Chenille
Hackle: Brown palmered
Head: Gray

Another favorite is the Gray-Brown Woolly Worm. I have used it in both lakes and streams to good effect. I usually favor sizes 8 to 12, depending upon what insects I think are present in the water. Although it does not produce as well as the darker woolly worm patterns, there are times when it can shine and so is always in my travelling fly box for immediate use. The Gray-Brown Woolly Worm should be worked in lakes extremely slowly with the slightest twitches to give it a subtle, erratic fish-attracting movement. In streams it can be weighted and bounced or rolled along the bottom where fish mistake it for any number of good food items.

Olive Woolly Worm

Body: Olive
Hackle: Olive
Head: Brown

I use this pattern in both a size 8 and 12 but the smaller one brings in more trout that measure close to four pounds. This pattern can be tied fully if you like it that way—but don't get carried away.

You may be glad to know that this pattern is for shallow and weedy areas. (At least, it seems to be more effective in depths from three to eight feet.) The pattern works well because weed beds are green and insects which inhabit them are also olive in color. In these shallows, a long leader on a floating line works well.

Short and jerky line strips seem to work best. I would use a size 12 in the spring and summer and then go up to a size 8 when the browns move into the shallows late in the fall.

Slower, more even strips, seem to work better beneath five feet or at the point where the food shelf dips sharply toward the depths.

Another situation where the Olive Woolly works well is in greenish water—but the Brown Woolly works better. With either color when fishing such water, the retrieve should be slow and a bit erratic. Here, I still stick to a size 12 since it catches the most, and only the best trout!

The Olive Woolly Worm is tailor-made for spring and for use in limestone creeks, but the fly should be tied rather slimly and sparsely when fishing these slow and even currents. Late spring seems to be the time when many spring creek insects are the right color for this pattern. Without any weight and with a floating line and a long leader of up to 12 feet (in the biggest rivers), these will work well in even currents.

I'd cast across and up-current and let the fly sink slowly toward the bottom. In these waters, one can often observe the fly drifting to and then upon the bottom. It is very delicate work—most particularly when a big brown or rainbow trout cruises up to the Woolly. When this happens, with nerves of steel, let the fly drift a bit more and just barely dart the fly toward one side. The trout either takes the fly or backs up. With too much action from the fly, the fish may hurry to its hidden lair off in some dark corner of the river. I have observed this nymphing method by masters of the long rod and it works every time. Don't ask about my results!

If a trout doesn't show up on the scene, finish the cross-stream drift, carefully raise the line, make a new cast and slowly work various lanes of current. Drift the Woolly into places where a trout ought to be—near a stump, log, timber or weeds. Such cover found in midstream is the best.

I do my best work when I can't see the bottom—like in a lake. I slowly move along and probe the most likely spots. Without seeing the cruising trout, my nerves are probably better!

The Olive Woolly, at least for me, is not very effective in the rush of freestone currents but if I were to try it, I'd fish it like a typical wet fly.

As a bait fisherman, Izaak Walton wrote of caterpillars. In the fifth edition of his book, Charles Cotton wrote of the Palmer Fly otherwise known as the Woolly Worm. The connection between the two was probably a modern angler and neither Cotton nor Walton.

Hare's Ear

Tail: Brown hackle fibers
Rib: Fine brass tinsel
Body: Fur of hare's ear
Wing: Light gray duck quill
Head: Light brown
Tail: Brown hackle fiber

The Hare's Ear is (or has been) the best and all-time favorite standard wet fly pattern. Our current trend for strict imitations and nearly 100 variations of one pattern is the obvious reason for why it, and other winged wet flies, are not often found in the catalogs. If the various catalog companies were to carry only one of the winged wet fly patterns, it ought to be the Hare's Ear. In the Orvis catalog, I found it in three sizes—10, 12 and 14. An Eastern pattern, Orvis is the right company to sell it.

The applications are endless. Here, I will write only of the very best.

From the top of the water to the bottom is a logical technique. The winged Hare's Ear can be fished almost like a dry fly as well though. Out in a lake, I've caught many rising rainbow trout on this pattern whether they were feeding on a sparse hatch of mayflies—or caddisflies. In a size 16, it should be cast inches short of the rise and then quickly darted just under the surface.

The main requirement is a nine- or 10-foot leader tapered to 4X and then the floating line. If the trout does not hit, keep the fly just under the surface by bringing it back in short and erratic strips.

In a lake, more then a few feet under the surface, trout want nymphs, woollies or streamers—not winged wet flies. In a stream, though, the Hare's Ear is in its glory. My thought is that the wing or feather of a wet fly is worked best by currents rather than by one's hand.

Cast a size 14 Hare's Ear straight across the current. Follow the drift with the rod tip. Lightly dart it as the line straightens out below you. With a floating line and a 10-foot leader, the fly can reach four-or five-foot depths on its own power. If it's necessary to get the fly down deeper, use the very smallest of split shot just above the eye of the hook. Otherwise, the natural action of the fly is spoiled. The fly, at the end of the drift, should be darted not upstream but to the left or right and toward other lanes of current. Point the rod tip in the desired direction.

In a pool or in flat areas with good cover, first cast upstream to quickly get the fly (on its own power) to the bottom and then dart it a bit faster than the current. In quiet spots like these, a size 16 works best.

In a riffle, this method also works well. Here, a size 12 or a size 14 Hare's Ear works when it is cast upstream and darted straight across the currents. Bring it back toward where you stand.

In small streams, the leader ought to be at least six feet long and tapered to 4X or 6X. The smallest of brooks are restricted pretty much to bow and arrow casts, three-foot level leaders and a quick drift.

In deep runs and large freestone rivers, a Wet Tip works well with a five-foot, 2X level leader and a size 6 or 8 Hare's Ear. The floating section needs to be continually mended upstream to give the fly a drag-free drift. I'd probably use the size 8 Hare's Ear since it seems better in the various types of water. Scour the bottoms of runs, riffles and sliding currents with upstream casts. Feel for the moment when the line scrapes the rocks or boulders. That is the time to jerk the fly across the currents. This strongly resembles streamer fishing. A size 6 is probably the maximum wet fly size, as a size 16 is probably the minimum.

In the days of Charles Cotton, this wet fly was used as a general purpose pattern to imitate a group of sedges (which is an older term for caddisflies). The nymph came probably in Hewitt's mid-life.

Black Ant

Body: Two humps of black thread barely separated
with a black hackle

Ants are likely to be the most prevalent of all insects and they can be found in almost any terrain. When currents are muddy from a short thunderstorm, some ants (and other terrestrial insects) are pummeled into the stream from bank side cover.

With a size 12 Black Ant on the leader, fish it a few inches under the surface by casting above the mud line and drifting it well below it. Hits are delicate and light. I honestly believe that a slow action rod helps detect a light strike. It also helps absorb the angler's sometimes excited response.

Drift the ant through the muddy section and on into clear water. It's important to carefully present the fly, and line, lightly to the surface since ant-feeding trout are easily spooked. In fast currents, the muddy stain usually dissipates in about an hour. Fish it slowly for at least half that time. Nothing in our sport is a guarantee but this method works often enough to make it worthwhile. After the ant, try a black cricket or grasshopper pattern as a wet fly. Fish them in the same way.

The same storm tends to put pasture creek trout on the bottom. A size 14 or a size 16 Black Ant fished at the level of the trout should work. (Black is good to begin with when one is new to the river but listening to a local expert is even better!) Do not use weight or any sort of sinking line. If more depth is necessary, lengthen the leader and cast further upstream. My time spent at Hat Creek, the Yellow Breeches, and even the tail waters of the San Juan River made these principles of anting very clear.

Ant-feeding trout require careful casting and quiet presentations.

In a lake, at least for trout, forget this pattern until there is a strong hatch. Here though, at least out West, it will be the Flying Ant which is best fished as a dry fly.

The Black Ant pattern is very close to the original which goes back to the 16th century when Cotton and Walton used those 16-foot reel-less rods and dappled their flies on the surface.

Coachman

Tag: Gold tinsel
Body: Peacock herl
Wing: White duck quill
Hackle: Red-brown cock

In moving currents, a size 12 Coachman wet fly makes an excellent exploratory pattern. With a floating line and a long leader, cast it up and across the currents. The idea is to jerk the fly down toward, and into, the depths. Continue with this erratic retrieve until the fly is straight across from you. At that point, quickly strip it across the currents and toward where you're standing. (This method works well for a deep wading angler.) Less intrepid fly fishers should let the fly drift down the river toward ideal fish cover. Random casts and drifts are seldom effective. (The very best anglers read the water before making a single cast.)

I think of any white-winged pattern as an "attractor". It guides my fishing methods.

In the riffle of a creek, cast a size 14 Coachman straight upstream and dart it back down just a bit faster than the current. In big rivers, full of rocks and boulders, with a Sink Tip and a five-foot 2X tippet, clamp a split shot at the eye of a size 8 Coachman and cast it across the currents. Jerk it across the river when you begin to feel the fly bounce off the rocks. Another technique is to cast a size 12 Coachman down and across a run. Hurry it back upstream.

The Coachman and these various methods will work well in any freestone stream, but they will have little effect in meandering currents.

In the trout lakes of the West, I have found that the wet Coachman is almost useless no matter how I fished it.

An English coachman, Tom Bosworth, created this wet fly. Although it was developed and tested in England, it became one of the most popular wet fly patterns here in the United States up through, at least, the 1940s.

Dry Flies

Adams

Tail: Golden pheasant tippet fibers
Body: Dark blue dun mole's fur dubbing
Wings: Dark grizzle hackle points
Hackle: A natural red-brown and grizzle cock hackle
wound together

The Adams is a universal pattern which works on any type of river almost anywhere in this country, or the world for that matter! It can resemble a mosquito, caddis, mayfly dun, midge or horsefly. Carry sizes ranging from a 10 to a 20. Larger patterns wouldn't hurt either if you have the room.

It shines as an exploratory pattern. In a size 12 or 14, cast it upstream and let the fly naturally drift in the current. There are many ways to do this. The simplest and easiest is usually overlooked. (Serpentine or curve casts are fun and have their place but they are not always necessary.) With a short cast and a high rod, keep the line straight in the air as the fly drifts downstream. You only need to move the rod with the speed of the current. With thumb and forefinger, keep tension on the line. Lightly strike with those fingers when a trout slurps up the fly. Too much of a snap will whip the fly out of the trout's lip. For this sort of fishing, eight to nine-foot rods are helpful.

Extend the natural drift of the fly by lowering the rod to let the Adams float down the river below you. It's always important to maintain tension on the line. With the rod, the fly can be directed toward bank cover. Let the current hop the fly toward the desired target. Never use the fingers. They tend to be too quick! Remember the trout's natural habit is to run upstream after feeling the sting of the hook. Upon a strike, lift the rod and quickly reel up the slack line. This method adds spice to a day of fishing.

Attractor fishing is possible with the Adams. The idea is to advertise the fly and entice a trout to come up for it. With a slight twitch, the fly can skip about or momentarily dip into the film. I have not mastered this tactic since there is a very fine line between good natural movement, and too much. (This is a possible method for trout cruising near a food shelf in a lake when there is no real concentration of a hatch.)

Serpentine and curve casts over 30 feet long, will become important. This is usually when fishing a large river whose currents twist about in a strange web.

In a meadow creek, the Adams chosen should be from a size 16 to a size 20. Natural drifts with the current are good for exploring, or in a hatch of almost any gray or dark fly. Sometimes, the non-match theory works best.

Placid currents require at least a nine-foot leader and a 4X tippet. A 6X and a 12-foot leader is better when slow currents are bright and clear. Even in tumbling waters, dry fly fishermen should go no heavier than a 2X.

Len Halliday is the tier who developed the Adams. In 1922, he named it for an Ohio attorney who spent one summer on Arbutus Lake and christened the pattern in the Boardman River. They are two of Michigan's best underrated trout waters.

Ray Bergman may be one of the earliest to write of it.

Light Cahill

Tail: Pale ginger cock hackle fibers
Body: Cream fox fur dubbing
Wings: Flanks of wood-duck or mandarin
Hackle: Grizzle cock hackle

The Light Cahill dry fly should be used toward the end of the day since its light shade makes it easy to see as darkness comes on. It also strongly resembles mayfly hatches which take place from May until July on Eastern rivers and from June to July on Western ones. The fly should be cast upstream and drifted down with the current. At the end of the float, lift the line, false cast once or twice, and drop the Cahill into another lane of current. Riffles and quiet slides of current are perfect for this technique. Always remember to cast ahead of a rising trout.

Ten-foot, 4X leaders work well with size 12 or size 14 patterns. During the day, a size 16 might be better.

Thinking "ideal" for a moment, one could take a medium outfit like a 6 or 7 weight fly rod, walk a long way down, or upstream, and work back to the car and switch to a lighter rod for the quiet spots in the opposite direction. By always working back toward the car, you save leg power for wading and fishing! It is a good way to fish different spots with different types of tackle and adds variety to the day. (I read of this idea long ago.)

The Light Cahill is perfect for spring creeks. With a size 16 pattern, I'd stick to the natural upstream drifts.

In general, the pattern imitates any cream-colored mayfly—in particular some of the duns of the Pale Evening Dun, the Little Yellow May and wind-blown duns of the *Callibaetis*.

In his streamside guide, Art Flick calls the Light Cahill the one pattern everyone has.

Theodore Gordon seems to be the originator of the pattern but today's dressing came to us from Mr. William Chandler of Neversink, New York. Gordon preferred heavier materials for his dry flies.

Dark Cahill

Tail: Red-brown cock hackle fibers
Body: Gray muskrat fur dubbing
Hackle: Natural red-brown cock
Wings: Flank of drake wood-duck of mandarin

By carrying these first three patterns—the Adams, and the Light and Dark Cahills—from a size 12 to a size 20, a huge number of hatches from every border of our country are well imitated. These "big three" dry flies cover the basic three insect shades of gray, yellow and brown. The main exception would be caddis and stoneflies.

Here's another approach with this basic color scheme. Explore a stream at dawn with a size 12 or a size 14 Dark Cahill, during the day with the Adams and near twilight with the Light Cahill. Such exploring with these delicate patterns is best in riffles, sliding runs and quiet stretches.

In 25- to 35-foot wide streams, the best tactic for the Dark Cahill is to make an upstream cast and let it float naturally with the current. The "real" dry fly artists spend more time drifting the fly in the currents and less time with wide loops in the air.

Like its light cousin, the Dark Cahill shines its best in slow meadow streams. In tumbling currents, I might use one in a size 12 but I would drop down to a size 16 in pools and quiet holes. Avoid tailouts and flats during the day unless you notice trout in them but that is rare. In 60-plus foot rivers, I would let the fly drift to some point opposite me and then cast again. Yet, the Dark Cahill works when it is skim-jerked across the currents at that point. It might look like an erupting caddis when fished in this fashion.

When tied with thick hackles, the Dark Cahill works well in heavy currents. Apparently, its silhouette is more noticeable than lighter-colored patterns. For this method, I would switch to a size 12 or a size 10 fly. On long casts, the serpentine or curve casts are effective in a myriad of currents.

The Dark Cahill is most imitative of the dark Quill mayflies or gray drakes which usually hatch in early summer.

This pattern was originated by Dan Cahill after Theodore Gordon invented the Light version. The parachute forms are modern and make for good exploratory patterns.

Bivisible

Tail: Hackle tips
Hackle: White tied at head followed by two stiff
cock hackles of desired color

The Bivisible is among the most versatile of all dry flies since it can be used in any type of river or lake. It is only a matter of choosing the best size, style and shade. The most common colors are brown, gray and black. These three Bivisibles imitate the bulk of the caddis and stonefly hatches. The fly can be tied as large as a size 4 for heavy currents and stonefly hatches, and as small as a size 16 for placid waters and tiny caddisfly hatches. A size 10 or a size 12 might be the most useful but, as a die-hard float tuber, I would probably use a size 12 or a size 14 most frequently. A lightly hackled Bivisible has a better effect in placid currents while the heaviest type takes more of a beating in frothy currents. The type bought in stores and catalogs will be reasonable in both situations.

Most often, Bivisibles are used in bouncy to moderate currents. This is one pattern which can be drifted for the whole length of the drift—from the farthest upstream point to the opposite end of the cast. In fact, line can be pulled out to extend the downstream float but it is important to keep it drag-free. Although I still haven't quite mastered it, an upstream twitch on the line at the end of the drift can bring amazing results—if one can lead the fly to a trout, or where one ought to be. The tactic might wake-up resting trout or change the mind of feeding one too. This little line strip can also be used at any time but it is more effective on the downstream side of the drift.

In the slow sliding currents of a pasture river, the Bivisible must be small. A size 16 is about right—even if a short-striking trout misses it. (I hate that!) In quiet waters, a Bivisible flattened on one side and riding flush on the surface, will result in success too. It makes the fly look more like a caddisfly. Dead-drift this altered fly. It is better without the twitch.

The Bivisible is one of the best flies for stillwaters. During a light wind, it can be drifted along the surface and over a weedy food shelf where trout are likely to rest near the bank. I need an intense hatch and concentration of rising trout to move me from deep water though.

When E. R. Hewitt invented the pattern to dry fly fish his section of the Neversink River, he wanted an attractor floating fly.

Compared to other patterns, it is fairly new since he gave it life early in our century.

Irresistible

Tail: Dark deer hair from body of white-tail deer
Body: Dark gray clipped deer hair
Wing: White-tail deer hair of same color
Hackle: Dusty rusty dun cock hackle

The Irresistible is the thickest pattern listed in this book and its bulk has advantages.

The one advantage that I like most, is to think of the fly as a trout "bass bug". When I think, or know, that trout are near shoreline cover, I'll tie one on in a size 10 or a size 12 and cast it to likely spot. Tiny line jerks advertise it well. The method also works during a hatch.

It is also perfect as an exploratory pattern on a stream for when trout are not rising. In creeks, it should be in a size 12 or a size 14 and fished with upstream drifts in the faster stretches. In larger rivers, a size 8 or a size 10 gives a better profile for the heavier currents. In any case, trout savagely hit it.

A size 10 or a size 12 will be good at night in a meadow stream. Drift it close to a known trout hideout and twitch it once or twice. Night is no time for exploring or fancy casting. Find a good spot and move as little as necessary. Keep wading to a minimum.

Balderdash the trout by pinching some split shot half a foot up the leader and by fishing the Irresistible as a wet fly through heavy currents. Here, of course, it becomes something like a lure! It is said to work well but be sure it is legal!

Either Joe Messinger (of West Virginia) or Harry Darbee (of Livingston Manor, New York) originated this pattern during the 1930s. The subject is a bit controversial.

Hair Wing Royal Coachman

Tail: Golden pheasant tippets
Body: In three equal parts: peacock herl, scarlet silk floss, and peacock herl
Wings: White calf tail hair
Hackle: Natural red-brown cock hackle

The Hair Wing Royal Coachman, although made for riffles, runs and rushing currents also can have an effect if used in long slow and deep runs. Its brightness attracts many warm water species as well as trout. On a slow dry fly day during the summer, tie a size 14 Hair Wing Royal Coachman on the tippet and cast it straight across a placid current. Let it drift a moment and then twitch it. As it glides downstream (and along a weed line), lift the line to keep it drag-free and carefully twitch it several times throughout the drift. The slight bobbing of the dry fly can turn things around. It can also be fished this way along a weed line, near rocks, or sunken timber, when a light wind ruffles the surface of a lake—but deep water must be nearby.

The Royal Coachman Hair Wing shines its best in "rougher" currents of a freestone river. Learn how to notice breaks and bumps which designate spots where underwater currents slow down. Such quiet areas designate underwater cover. These are the spots where the biggest trout will be.

The fly should be cast upstream and bubbled along downstream for the whole length of the drift. Lightly twitch the fly the moment it bounces near a known trout lair.

It is a perfect pattern to tie on when learning a river. Without a hatch, a size 14 or a size 16 Hair Wing Royal Coachman is not only easy to see, but also looks like a slightly drowned mayfly.

Lee Wulff's Royal Wulff dry fly pattern is very similar to the Hair Wing Royal Coachman. Both would be fished exactly the same way and for the same reasons.

The original Coachman was first tied as a wet fly in 1878 by John Haily, a professional tier who lived in New York City.

The Dry Fan Wing variety came about during the days of Ray Bergman either in the 1930s or 40s.

In 1929, L. Q. Quackenbush wondered if fly tier Reuben Cross would consider using upright white wings of calf tail and tail fibers of natural brown bucktail. He did and we know the results. The local Catskill anglers soon called it the Quack Coachman. Once it became widely known to western anglers, the fly was given its descriptive name and—history was made!

Elk Hair Caddis

Body: Dubbed hare's ear mask
Hackle: Brown palmered throughout the body
Rib: Fine copper wire
Wing: Tan elk hair
Head: Stubs of elk hair wing

Brown, olive, gray and tan cover at least 75percent of the colors found in most hatches and the Elk Hair Caddis comes in all of these shades. (Caddisfly flies range from size 4 to 22.) The average angler can probably get away with the middle range from a size 10 to a size 16.

The size 12 (or a size 14) of the Elk Hair Caddis makes a great exploratory pattern. In fast currents, cast it upstream and across. Bounce it in the surface layer as the fly begins its downstream drift. On the downward trek, mend the line upstream and lightly bob the fly once again. Remember, think cover.

When targeting a feeding trout, remember to cast ahead of it and drift the fly toward it. Keep the line short, tight and out of the water. Barely twitch the fly as it inches close to the trout.

With a caddis imitation like this one, concentrate on fast rocky sections since the bulk of them reside in such water. If it fails (particularly during a hatch) tie on an exact winged imitation like the Slow Water Caddis. (There is also another one called the Delta Wing.) They are important patterns for pools and placid smooth runs. As currents slow down to bubbly runs and riffles, a size 14 is better but a size 16 is usually the best for pools and other slow spots.

The same patterns work in quiet bodies of water. Yet, I would start with the Elk Hair Caddis in a size 16 since it twitches better. In stillwaters, it takes a serious hatch to bring the trout up. The fly is cast to a riser. After I take a quick breath, I twitch the fly quietly. Either a trout snaps it up or fins its way to cover. One can wait for another riser and cast to it, or bubble the fly back to boat or tube. Casting toward the bank works best.

For many years, palmered flies like the Bivisible were the only caddisfly imitations. The exact winged ones have come about during the last 15 years or so. Leonard M. Wright Jr. and Gary LaFontaine are two of the best-known pioneers for caddisfly imitations used for fly fishing. The originator for this particular fly was Al Troth.

Dave's Hopper

Tail: Red deer hair fibers with small loop of yellow yarn
Body: Yellow yarn
Body hackle: Brown palmered, then clipped
Underwing: Yellow kip tail
Overwing: Two turkey quill wing sections
Legs: Yellow grizzly hackle stems clipped and knotted
Head: Deer hair spun and clipped

There are too many varieties of this large terrestrial imitation. Dave's Hopper, with a trimmed hair wing head, is one of the most popular. (I'd opt for the trimmed bucktail head of Dave's Hopper but the demanding trout of meandering creeks require the other one.) With the bucktail head pattern, I can explore currents with it and fish during "Hoppertunity" time—but I have never found it in California or in the lakes of Arizona.

The best idea is to head to a river known for such activity in late June or July. Although the pattern can be used to explore side currents undulating near weed lines, it works the best when trout are lined near the bank as when hungry folks stand in a cafeteria line. Fish Dave's Hopper by lightly slapping the fly just ahead of the trout hugging the bank and let it drift down with the current. If walking the bank, one must step very lightly. A good wading fly rodder works the same way.

The best Hopper anglers stick to short casts.

One might move from one trout to the next. Either the rainbow or brown attacks the fly or it goes under the surface—but not far. (Grasshoppers to trout, are like prime rib for us.)

When exploring, cast near something. Hoppers are not a fly to be indiscriminately cast about. Look for shady areas, stumps, weeds, etc. The 2X tippet and the seven to nine-foot leader are usually sufficient. False casting should be minimal. A weight-forward floating line might be needed for Dave's Hopper. Big ones are bulky.

The Letort Hopper is likely to be the first tied specifically for the Grasshopper. It takes us back to Charles Fox and Vincent Marinaro but Dave Whitlock is usually credited for the popularity and great success for the detailed grasshopper imitations.

Black Fur Ant

Body: Two humps of fur between a light hackle

Most of the time, ant-feeding trout are finicky. The imitation must be the right color and size. Although black is the most common shade, they can also be brown, gray, red and tan. Some are too tiny to imitate though. Yet, they can be quite large—particularly out West.

Tied to float flush on the film, the ant is strictly for times when trout are looking upward and feeding on those minuscule insects.

The flying ant is a large Western white-winged insect. It swarms to lakes usually in late May or early June. The imitation should be on a size 12 or a size 10 hook.

Cast it gently and directly in front of a trout's nose. Inch the fly forward. Let it sit still until you know which trout to target next and repeat the steps. It's a simple technique but also very meticulous. The ant is fished in the film—not above or below it.

A size 20 is probably the best over-all size. To be reasonably confident, it's good to also carry ants in a size 16 and a size 12. I'm not sure of the worth of ants tied smaller than a size 20.

A 10-foot leader with at least a two-foot strand of 6X tippet and a soft-action rod are mandatory for successful ant dry fly fishing. At times, a longer leader—down to an 8X—is necessary. With Orvis, it tests at 1.75 pounds. I have managed with my parabolic 7 weight outfit but a 5 or 4 weight one is much better. It presents the fly softly with more ease and absorbs hard strikes much better. Anything lighter is not necessary.

Use the same method in a pool or a meadow creek. One must cast upstream and to a particular trout. Keep the line almost straight in the current. Let it move the fly. Casts should be few and gently brought down. Even well-advanced anglers can mess things up so don't feel bad. One must keep nerves steady when observing two-foot trout casually sipping up these minuscule creatures.

Timing must be perfect to find anting trout. Usually, the air is almost hot when they either fly to the surface of a lake or get swept into it. The exact part of the season, or day, varies too much from river to river and region to region. They nearly always stay in subtle currents and in sunny areas.

The best thing is to fish every weekend and stumble on it!

In the 1930s, both Edward R. Hewitt and Ray Bergman experimented with ant patterns. Hewitt tried a winged pattern while Bergman developed a cork-bodied one. Hewitt did many things concerning ants including tasting them only to find that they were acidic. (His assumption is that trout taste things the same way as we do!)

Vince Mariano, Charles Fox, and Bob McCafferty confirmed the importance of terrestrials. In fact, they often worked together. McCafferty popularized the wet version of the Black Ant in the 1950s. Within 10 years or so, the floating type was available.

Black Midge
Tail: Black hackle fibers
Body: Black dubbing
Hackle: Black

Like ants, midges come in many shades but the Black Midge must be the most common.

In rivers, midges can occur anytime of the year—including in the winter! Some can be as large as a size 14. Most of the time, a size 20 or a size 22 will suffice yet "experts" tie midges down to a size 28! That makes me shudder!

Leaders need to be at least 10 feet long, if not more, and tippets should be 6X. As with the ants, casting and presenting these tiny things must be fastidious. One little error and you can scare a 12-inch trout. (In a riffle, the same leader can be reduced to nine feet.)

The presentation must be directly in front of a feeding trout. It is best not to move the fly. Ideally, the trout sucks it in. With a moving current, let the fly drift downstream. It is important to keep as much of the bulky fly line off the surface. The drift, though, cannot be too long. Any minor sort of drag on the fly, leader or line, ruins the hatch for everyone.

In a lake, don't wait too long or the tiny artificial will sink. One false cast will dry it. Each cast must be presented to a feeding trout. Hatches occur anytime on lakes or streams but, most of the time, I have found such hatches near twilight.

In summary, carry the Midge in black, gray and brown. Learn what local varieties dominate your area. Be discriminate on how they are fished.

May every angling day be productive and full of good times.

Index of Flies

Nymphs

Streamers and Bucktails

Wets

Dries